Child Anxiety & Screen Time

A 5-Step Plan to Support Kids with Anxiety and Create a Calmer Daily Rhythm

mf

Disclaimer

By reading this guide, you are accepting the terms of this disclaimer in full. If you do not agree with these terms, please do not read or use this guide.

All content within this guide is provided for informational and educational purposes only and should not be considered medical, psychological, or other professional advice. The author is not a doctor, physician, psychologist, psychotherapist, counselor, or licensed healthcare provider. Reading or using this guide does not establish any form of a patient-client or therapeutic relationship.

Always consult with a physician, licensed therapist, or other qualified health professional regarding any questions or concerns you may have about your physical or mental health. Never disregard professional advice or delay seeking it because of something you have read in this guide.

The information presented in this guide is based on general research, personal interpretation, and publicly available sources. While reasonable efforts have been made to provide accurate and current information, the author and publisher make no representations or warranties about the completeness, accuracy, reliability, or suitability of the content. The author and publisher shall not be held liable for any errors, omissions, or outcomes related to the use of this guide.

You acknowledge that you are solely responsible for how you choose to use the information in this guide and that any actions you take based on this content are undertaken at your own risk. The publisher shall not be liable for any loss, injury, or damages arising from the application of any information provided herein.

This guide does not promise or guarantee any specific result, outcome, or improvement in well-being, mental health, or nervous system regulation. Individual results may vary.

Where applicable, any tools, concepts, or names mentioned are the property of their respective owners and are used strictly for identification or illustrative purposes. Their mention does not imply endorsement. Any individuals shown in the cover or promotional images are stock photography models, and image rights have been obtained through appropriate licensing agreements.

Table of Contents

Introduction

Parenting is a beautiful journey filled with love, laughter, and unforgettable moments. Yet, it also comes with its share of challenges, especially when it comes to navigating the emotional well-being of your child. Today's world presents unique pressures for children. From the constant pull of digital devices and overstimulating environments to academic demands and social complexities, it's no wonder so many young minds feel overwhelmed.

For parents, managing these stressors while creating a peaceful family rhythm can feel daunting. The pervasive influence of screens, combined with packed schedules and rising expectations, often leaves families feeling rushed, disconnected, and uncertain about how best to help their kids. Yet, hope lies in intentional, actionable steps.

In this guide, we will talk about the following:

- Home What Anxiety Looks Like in Kids Today
- Root Causes of Anxiety in Children
- Five-Step Plan
- 30-Day Family Calm Plan

Keep reading to learn more about creating a peaceful family rhythm and helping your child manage anxiety. By the end of this guide, you will have the tools and resources to support your child's emotional well-being and create a more harmonious family dynamic.

What Anxiety Looks Like in Kids Today

In this chapter, we will discuss the prevalence of anxiety in children and how it manifests differently compared to adults. We will also explore common triggers and warning signs of anxiety in kids.

Understanding the Modern Landscape of Childhood Anxiety

Childhood anxiety is more common than many parents realize. Roughly one in five children experiences significant anxiety, meaning almost every classroom, park, or sports team has kids managing big worries. While it's normal for all children to feel fear or nervousness at times, shifts in modern life have made anxiety a more frequent and pervasive issue.

Today's kids face pressures that didn't exist a generation ago. Academic demands have increased, social connections often revolve around digital interactions, and kids are exposed to news and global crises at an earlier age. Add this to changes in family rhythms, like busier work schedules and less unstructured playtime, and it's clear why anxiety has taken root.

Unlike physical illnesses, anxiety isn't always easy to recognize. Children may not have the vocabulary to explain their feelings, so they express their worries differently. Instead of saying, "I feel anxious," a child might cry before school, complain of stomach discomfort after watching something upsetting, or suddenly refuse to do activities they previously enjoyed.

It's important to view these behaviors as signals asking for support. With the right guidance, children can learn to manage worries and thrive. The first step is recognizing how anxiety appears in their daily lives.

Why Support, Not Fixing, Is the Goal

As parents, it's natural to want to take away your child's pain immediately. When you see them struggle, you may feel the urge to jump in and eliminate the problem causing their distress. However, it's important to understand that anxiety isn't something to "fix" like a scraped knee. Instead, the goal is to provide support so your child feels empowered to handle their emotions.

Think of anxiety management as teaching a skill, not solving a crisis. When a child learns to recognize anxiety and apply coping strategies, they build lifelong resilience. Shielding them from every difficult situation may feel helpful in the short term, but it can prevent them from developing confidence in their ability to manage challenges.

For example, if your child worries about participating in a school performance, you might feel tempted to excuse them from it entirely. However, working with them to practice calming techniques and face their fear in small, manageable ways helps build their courage. It also teaches them that while worry is uncomfortable, it doesn't have to stop them from succeeding.

Your role as a parent is to guide, encourage, and model calm behaviors. Showing patience and acceptance helps children know that it's okay to struggle and that they can overcome difficulties with time and effort.

Common Symptoms by Age

Anxiety doesn't look the same across all ages. Children express their emotions in ways that align with their developmental stages. Below is a breakdown of common anxiety symptoms based on age group.

Preschoolers (Ages 3–5):

- Fear of separation from parents, often resulting in clinginess or crying when dropped off for daycare or preschool.
- Frequent nightmares or fears of the dark.

- Avoidance of unfamiliar people or settings.
- Meltdowns that seem disproportionate to the situation.
- Regressive behaviors like thumb-sucking or bedwetting.

Elementary-Age Children (Ages 6–11):

- Complaints about physical issues, like stomachaches, headaches, or fatigue, with no apparent medical cause.
- They are reluctant to try new activities or avoid things they perceive as difficult.
- Asking repetitive questions about safety or routines (e.g., "What if something bad happens at school?").
- Perfectionism or becoming easily frustrated when things don't go as planned.
- Trouble sleeping due to worry about upcoming events.

Teenagers (Ages 12–18):

- Increased irritability, mood swings, or emotional outbursts.
- Avoidance of social situations, opting to spend more time alone.
- Procrastination or refusal to engage in challenging tasks due to fear of failure.
- Frequent self-criticism or verbal statements like "I'm not good enough."
- Physical symptoms, such as tension headaches or muscle soreness.

By identifying these signs, parents and caregivers can take the first step toward supporting their children's emotional needs.

The Hidden Signs Parents Often Miss

Some signs of anxiety are subtle and can easily be misinterpreted as a child "acting out" or "being difficult." These hidden signals often go unnoticed until they begin interfering with daily routines. Recognizing them can help parents respond more effectively.

One common hidden sign is trouble concentrating. A child who seems distracted might be internally preoccupied with worry, rather than simply lacking focus. For example, a child staring out the window during class might be rehearsing a feared situation in their mind rather than ignoring the teacher.

Another often-missed sign is physical tension. Anxiety can present as restlessness, fidgeting, or even small habits like nail-biting or hair-twirling. These behaviors stem from a need to release the body's physical energy built up by worry.

Perfectionism is another subtle signal. A child who becomes overly frustrated by their mistakes might be driven by a deep fear of failure or criticism. While this may seem like high motivation on the surface, it often hides an intense mental struggle.

Lastly, withdrawal is easily overlooked, particularly in older children or teens. A child who starts spending significantly more time in their room or avoids family activities might be retreating because of worries they feel unable to share.

By observing these subtle behaviors closely, parents can get a clearer picture of their child's internal experience.

When Worry Becomes a Pattern

It's normal for children to feel anxious occasionally, especially when they face new or potentially overwhelming situations. Starting at a new school, studying for a big test, or encountering conflicts with peers are all typical triggers of temporary anxiety.

However, when occasional worry turns into a consistent pattern, it may indicate a deeper issue. For example, if a child repeatedly refuses to attend school or avoids social settings entirely, these behaviors suggest chronic anxiety that requires attention.

Repeated avoidance is especially important to address. While avoiding a feared situation can provide immediate relief, it reinforces the idea that the situation is unsafe. Over time, avoidance can limit a child's ability to engage fully in life, trapping them in cycles of fear. Identifying these patterns early allows parents to intervene and support their child with appropriate tools.

When you notice worry becoming a routine, reflect on how it's affecting daily life. ***Questions to consider include***:

- Is worry preventing your child from doing activities they once loved?
- Are physical complaints (like headaches) becoming more frequent?
- Is your child spending significant energy planning how to avoid certain situations?

If the answer is yes, it may be time to take a closer look. Once chronic anxiety patterns are identified, steps can be taken to address the underlying causes and help children regain their confidence.

By understanding what anxiety looks like, parents can take the crucial first step in supporting their child's emotional well-being. Recognizing patterns, paying attention to subtle signals, and focusing on support over fixing can provide children with the stability they need to face challenges. This foundation sets the stage for creating sustainable tools and habits that empower kids to thrive.

The Root Triggers

Understanding the root causes of anxiety in children requires looking beyond the symptoms. Anxiety is influenced by a combination of biological, environmental, and emotional factors that interact uniquely in each child.

By identifying and addressing these triggers, parents can create a supportive environment that helps reduce stress and fosters resilience. This chapter explores these foundational influences, offering practical advice to help parents manage and mitigate potential sources of anxiety.

Biological, Environmental, and Emotional Factors

Children are complex beings, and their anxiety can stem from multiple sources at once. These three categories often overlap, highlighting how interconnected the causes of anxiety can be.

Biological Factors

Some children are genetically predisposed to anxiety. If parents or close relatives have a history of anxiety or related conditions, the child may have inherited a heightened sensitivity to stress. This doesn't mean the child is destined to struggle, but it does mean they might require extra tools to self-regulate.

Additionally, the brain's chemistry plays a role. Kids with overactive amygdalas (the brain's fear center) may interpret relatively harmless situations as threats. This can make everyday challenges feel overwhelming.

Parents should also be aware of physical conditions that can exacerbate anxiety. For instance, children with sensory processing difficulties may feel overstimulated in noisy or crowded environments. Similarly, chronic illnesses can add a layer of stress that amplifies their emotional responses.

Environmental Factors

The world children grow up in shapes their emotional patterns, and today's fast-paced, high-pressure environment can be anxiety-inducing. External factors like academic expectations, exposure to world events, and social comparison (fueled by social media) all contribute.

Additionally, disruptions in physical environments, such as moving to a new home, family separations, or natural disasters, can lead to heightened stress. Since children thrive on predictability, sudden changes in their surroundings can make them feel insecure.

Emotional Factors

Children have varying levels of emotional sensitivity. Some kids are naturally more attuned to their feelings, which can make them react strongly to criticism, conflict, or perceived failure.

Parents should also consider their child's ability to process emotions. If emotional regulation wasn't modeled effectively at home, the child may struggle to self-soothe. Teaching kids how to label and work through feelings is crucial for building their ability to manage anxiety.

By assessing these biological, environmental, and emotional factors, parents can better understand what might be driving their child's anxiety and adjust their approach accordingly.

The Role of Screens, Sleep, and Nutrition

The everyday rhythms of a child's life significantly impact their mental health. Screens, sleep, and nutrition are three critical areas that either support or undermine emotional regulation. While they may seem like practical concerns, they're deeply connected to kids' well-being.

Screens and Anxiety

Technology has become a staple of daily life, but it comes with hidden costs for children. Excessive screen time, especially in the evening, overstimulates the brain and disrupts natural melatonin production, limiting the restorative benefits of sleep.

Screens can also expose children to stress-inducing content. Images of violence, scary scenarios, or even the pressures of curating a social media presence can heighten their anxiety. Additionally, the constant availability of notifications often keeps kids in a "fight or flight" mode as their minds anticipate what might happen next.

<u>To reduce the impact of screens:</u>

- ***Implement Tech-Free Zones***: Encourage screen-free times, especially during meals and before bed, to create spaces for connection and unwinding.
- ***Limit Interactive Use Before Sleep***: Avoid gaming, texting, or social apps right before bed since they stimulate the brain. Swap tech use with calming activities like reading or drawing.
- ***Model Healthy Screen Habits***: Kids mirror their caregivers. If parents set boundaries for their own screen usage, children are more likely to follow.

The Power of Sleep

Sleep is one of the most underrated tools for emotional resilience. Children need stable and sufficient sleep to regulate their moods, focus, and recharge. When sleep is disrupted, whether by anxiety, screen use, or inconsistent bedtime schedules, it creates a vicious cycle. Poor sleep increases irritability and worry, which, in turn, makes it harder for kids to fall asleep the following night.

To help support quality sleep:

- Set a Consistent Schedule: Research indicates that going to bed and waking up at the same time daily stabilizes circadian rhythms.
- Create a Wind-Down Routine: Help your child transition into rest with lower lights, calming activities, and no electronics in the hour leading up to bedtime.
- Address Physical Barriers: Ensure proper bedding, maintain a comfortable sleep temperature, and use white noise if background sounds are disruptive.

Nutrition as Emotional Fuel

What children eat has a major impact on their nervous system. An unbalanced diet can lead to blood sugar spikes and crashes, both of which can mimic or amplify feelings of anxiety. Nutrients like omega-3 fatty acids, magnesium, and complex carbohydrates help children feel calmer and more focused.

Practical tips for optimizing nutrition include:

- ***Avoid Over-Processed Foods***: While occasional treats are fine, diets high in sugar, artificial dyes, and caffeine can overstimulate the body and affect mood regulation.

- ***Encourage Regular Meals***: Skipping meals can lead to energy dips and increased irritability. Create a structure where snacks and meals occur at predictable times.
- ***Hydration Matters***: Even mild dehydration can contribute to fatigue and difficulty concentrating. Encourage water consumption throughout the day.

Balancing screens, sleep, and nutrition might feel overwhelming at first, but small, consistent adjustments can make a huge difference over time.

Family Dynamics and Pressure

The emotional environment at home profoundly affects children. Family tension, high expectations, and communication patterns all influence how children process and respond to stress. Even without realizing it, well-meaning families can unintentionally contribute to feelings of anxiety.

The Impact of Tension

Children are incredibly perceptive and often pick up on tensions between family members. Whether it's arguments, financial stress, or unspoken resentment, they may interpret these dynamics as unsafe, leading to a heightened sense of worry. Even when kids aren't directly involved in conflicts, witnessing them creates unease.

To foster a calmer atmosphere:

- ***Resolve Conflict Constructively***: Model respectful disagreement and prioritize resolution over blame.
- ***Reassure Through Connection***: Spend quality one-on-one time with your child, showing them they are safe and valued.
- ***Limit Over-Scheduling***: Overscheduling the family creates high-energy moments but leaves little time for rest. Balance activities with moments of peace.

Expectations and Pressure

Many kids feel overwhelming pressure to meet academic, athletic, or behavioral expectations. While encouragement is important, children should feel supported for who they are, not just for what they achieve.

Parents can help by:

- ***Promoting Effort Over Perfection***: Praise attempts rather than outcomes. For example, say, "I'm proud of how hard you worked on that project," rather than, "I'm glad you got an A."
- ***Creating Space for Failure***: Normalizing mistakes as a learning opportunity to reduce the fear of trying.
- ***Checking Your Own Expectations***: Sometimes, parents may unintentionally project their ambitions onto their child. Remind yourself that your child's path might look different from what you had envisioned.

Strengthening Communication Patterns

Open family dialogue encourages children to share their worries without fear of judgment. Ask how your child feels and listen actively without jumping to solutions right away. If they sense that their feelings are respected, they're more likely to approach you if anxiety arises.

By improving family dynamics and balancing expectations, you create a foundation where children feel supported, not pressured.

Understanding the root triggers of anxiety empowers parents to create targeted solutions. By addressing biological tendencies, optimizing practical areas like screens and sleep, and nurturing a calmer home dynamic, you can set up a solid foundation for your child to thrive emotionally. Identifying and adjusting these key areas can significantly reduce anxiety triggers and create an environment where resilience and confidence can grow.

Step 1 – Creating Safety Through Routine

Creating a routine is one of the simplest yet most powerful ways to lower anxiety in children. Routines help provide much-needed structure, offering kids a sense of safety and predictability in a world that often feels chaotic. By implementing steady and thoughtful routines, you're giving your child the grounding they need to feel more secure and focused.

Why Predictability Lowers Anxiety

For children who experience anxiety, an unpredictable day can feel overwhelming. Their minds might race with questions like, "What's going to happen next?" or "Will I be able to handle what's coming?" A structured routine eliminates many of these unknowns, offering reassurance and reducing worry.

When your child can anticipate what's next, they feel safer and more grounded. Predictability helps the brain relax because it signals stability. For example, if your child knows that every Monday they start the day with breakfast at the table and end with a family movie night, they'll begin to look forward to these rituals rather than fretting about the "what ifs."

Small, consistent habits also build emotional trust. Your child sees that you keep your word about routines, which reinforces their sense of safety. Over time, even moments of chaos (like rushing out the door) feel less stressful because the overarching framework remains steady.

Routines don't have to be complicated. It's about consistency, not perfection. Start with small rituals and build from there, giving your child the stability they need to flourish.

Morning and Bedtime Anchors

If your day feels chaotic from the start, that energy can ripple through the rest of it. Similarly, if bedtime is a stressful zone, it sets your child up for restless nights. Anchoring your child's day with clear morning and bedtime routines can create bookends of calm that promote peace and reduce anxiety throughout the day and night.

Morning Routines That Set the Tone

Mornings are your chance to set a positive tone for the entire day. A rushed or disorganized start can leave both you and your child feeling frazzled. But when mornings follow a predictable rhythm, they become opportunities to create calm and build confidence.

Here's an example of a simple, anxiety-reducing morning routine:

1. ***Wake at the Same Time Daily***: Try to keep wake-up times consistent during the week, even on weekends. This reinforces your child's natural sleep-wake cycle.
2. ***Connection First***: Spend a few moments connecting with your child before jumping into the day. A hug, a shared positive thought, or asking something like, "What are you looking forward to today?" can help create a sense of security.
3. ***Healthy Breakfast Choices***: Fuel their body and brain with nutritious food, like a bowl of oatmeal with fruit or scrambled eggs and whole-grain toast. Balanced meals can help regulate blood sugar, reducing irritability and anxious feelings.
4. ***Checklist for Independence***: If your child thrives on responsibility, use a checklist for the "must-dos" like brushing teeth, getting dressed, and packing a backpack. This gives them confidence and a sense of ownership over their morning.

Bedtime Routines That Calm the Mind

Bedtime often stirs up anxieties in kids. The quiet darkness gives their minds space to wander, which can lead to worries about the future or rehashing concerns from the day. A soothing bedtime routine acts as a mental and physical signal that it's time to transition into relaxation and sleep.

Here's how you can create a calming nighttime routine:

1. ***Wind Down Screen Use Early***: Turn off screens at least an hour before bed, as the blue light can interfere with their ability to fall asleep. Replace screens with quieter activities like puzzles, drawing, or reading.
2. ***Create a Structured Sequence***: Focus on doing the same three to four things in the same order each night, such as bath, pajamas, storytime, and cuddles. This repetition feels like a calming ritual.
3. ***Set the Scene for Sleep***: Keep their room cool, dimly lit, and free of clutter. If they're afraid of the dark, a nightlight with warm tones works well. Quiet sound machines or white noise can also help create a soothing environment.
4. ***Positive Reflections***: End the day on a high note by asking your child to share one good thing that happened. This encourages gratitude and helps shift their focus away from worries.

These routines not only help reduce bedtime battles but also set your child up for restorative sleep, which is key to managing anxiety.

Sample Daily Schedules

Your family's needs are unique, but sample schedules can serve as helpful starting points. Adjust them to work for your household while keeping consistency at the core.

For Preschoolers (Ages 3–5):

- ★ ***7 AM*** – Wake up, breakfast, and free-play time.
- ★ ***8 AM*** – Short learning activity or creative play (e.g., building blocks, coloring).
- ★ ***10 AM*** – Outdoor time (go to a park or play in the backyard).
- ★ ***12 PM*** – Lunch and quiet rest time.
- ★ ***2 PM*** – Imaginative play, storytime, or sensory activities (e.g., playdough, water play).
- ★ ***4 PM*** – Snack and wind-down outdoor game.
- ★ ***5 PM*** – Dinner with family.
- ★ ***7 PM*** – Bath, storytime, and bed by 7:30 PM.

For School-Age Kids (Ages 6–11):

- ★ ***7 AM*** – Wake up, breakfast, and get ready for school.
- ★ ***8 AM–3 PM*** – At school (or learning activities for homeschoolers).
- ★ ***3 PM*** – Snack, downtime, or outdoor play.
- ★ ***4 PM*** – Homework (split into short, focused sessions).
- ★ ***6 PM*** – Family dinner and connection time (discuss highs and lows of the day).

★ *7 PM* – Screen-free time (board games, reading, or hobbies).
★ *8 PM* – Bedtime routine starts. Bed by 8:30 PM.

For Teens (Ages 12–18):

★ *6 AM* – Wake up, quick breakfast, and organize their day.
★ *7 AM–3 PM* – School hours.
★ *3 PM* – Downtime or extracurricular activity.
★ *5 PM* – Homework (break into manageable chunks, set a timer for focus).
★ *6 PM* – Family dinner and open conversation.
★ *7 PM* – A mix of downtime and socializing (with limited or managed screen time).
★ *9 PM* – Prepare for bed (journaling, light reading). Bed by 9:30–10 PM.

By creating a structure tailored to your child's stage of development, you're helping them build habits that foster security and peace.

Routines don't just organize your child's day; they create a foundation of trust and safety. They provide the predictability your child's brain craves, helping to lower overall stress and foster emotional regulation. Start simple, adjust as you go, and watch how these small habits lead to a more harmonious home.

Step 2 – Calming Communication

When your child feels anxious, they often look to you for guidance, comfort, and reassurance. How you respond in these moments can either help them feel grounded or unintentionally escalate their worries. The words you choose, along with your tone and body language, play a powerful role in shaping how your child processes and manages their emotions.

This chapter will help you discover effective ways to communicate with your child during anxious moments. By focusing on calming language, addressing worries without amplifying them, and striking the right balance between validating and over-attending to their concerns, you can become a steady source of comfort and confidence for your child.

Phrases that De-escalate vs. Escalate

Your words have the power to soothe or intensify a stressful moment. Sometimes, in an effort to help, well-meaning phrases can make a child feel dismissed or more overwhelmed. Paying attention to how you phrase your responses can create an environment where your child feels heard and supported.

Here's a breakdown of common escalating versus de-escalating phrases:

Escalating:

- "Why are you so nervous about this? It's not a big deal."
- "You're overreacting. Calm down."
- "There's no reason to feel this way. Just stop worrying."
- "If you don't stop crying, we're going to leave."

These kinds of statements, even if said with good intentions, can make a child feel misunderstood, judged, or ashamed of their feelings. They may also discourage them from sharing their worries in the future.

De-escalating:

- "I see this is really tough for you right now."
- "It's okay to feel nervous. I've felt that way before too."
- "I'm here to help. Can we work through this together?"
- "Take your time. We can figure this out when you're ready."

De-escalating phrases show empathy and create a safe space for your child. They acknowledge the difficulty of the moment while reinforcing that they're not alone. With time, these calming responses can help your child feel more confident about facing challenges, knowing they have your support.

When speaking, keep your tone calm and your body language open. A soft voice, relaxed posture, and steady eye contact all reinforce the message that you're a safe anchor in their moment of stress.

How to Talk About Worries (Without Making Them Bigger)

When your child brings up a worry, your initial reaction might be to provide reassurance immediately. While this instinct is understandable, focusing too much on the worry itself can unintentionally make it feel larger and more intimidating. The key is to guide your child in processing their feelings without dwelling on them.

Here's how you can approach these conversations thoughtfully:

1. **Acknowledge the Feeling**

   Start by naming what you observe in a neutral, empathetic way. For example, if your child is upset about an upcoming school presentation, you might say, "It sounds like you're feeling nervous about speaking in front of the class."

This simple act of naming the emotion helps your child feel understood and reduces the intensity of the feeling. It also teaches them how to identify their own emotions more clearly.

2. **Avoid Reinforcing the Fear**

   While it's important to validate your child's concern, try not to overemphasize it. For instance, instead of asking, "Are you really worried this won't go well?" which keeps the focus on the negative outcome, shift the conversation toward problem-solving. Say, "What part of the presentation do you feel most confident about?" This subtle redirection encourages them to see the worry in a less all-encompassing way.

3. **Encourage Small Steps**

   Break big worries into manageable chunks for your child. If they're anxious about attending a new activity, you might say, "What's one thing we can do to make this feel easier? Would it help to watch a video about the activity or meet the teacher first?" Small, actionable steps reduce the fear of the unknown and help build coping skills.

4. **Use Open-Ended Questions**

   Ask thoughtful, guiding questions to better understand their perspective without leading them toward worry.

Instead of "What's making you so scared?" try, "What do you think would make this feel better?" Open-ended questions empower your child to share their thoughts and focus on solutions rather than dwelling on problems.

By shaping discussions this way, you're helping your child learn that while worries are uncomfortable, they don't have to control the situation. You're teaching them that their feelings are valid but manageable.

Validating Without Over-Attending

Validation is an essential tool in calming communication, but it's also a balancing act. If you invalidate your child's feelings by dismissing them, they may feel alienated. On the other hand, if you overly engage with their fears, you risk reinforcing the idea that the worry deserves all their attention.

Why Both Extremes Can Backfire

- ***Dismissal***: If you brush off their concerns with "You'll be fine, don't worry," they might feel like their feelings don't matter or that something must truly be wrong since you're not addressing it seriously.
- ***Over-Attention***: If you repeatedly revisit the worry, asking, "Are you still nervous about that?" or "What if it happens again?" you may inadvertently reinforce the idea that your fear is too big to overcome.

How to Validate Effectively

1. ***Acknowledge, Then Redirect***: You can show you understand their feelings while shifting the focus toward empowerment. For example, say, "I can tell this is really bothering you, but I know you can handle it with some practice. What's one thing we can do to help you feel more ready?"
2. ***Keep It Short and Simple***: Long conversations about anxiety can unintentionally amplify it. Focus on a brief acknowledgment, like, "I hear you're feeling worried. It's okay to have those feelings," and then move on to an action or distraction.
3. ***Focus on Confidence Over Comfort***: Instead of saying, "Don't worry, I'll handle it," try, "This is hard, but I believe in you. I know you've faced tough things before, and you'll do great." Encouraging self-reliance builds long-term resilience.

Create Healthy Coping Patterns

Help your child shift their focus from the worry itself to useful calming tools. If they're upset, encourage them to try a coping activity, like deep breathing, jumping on a trampoline, or coloring a picture. This not only helps in the moment but also teaches them strategies they can use independently as they grow.

The Art of Balanced Presence

It’s important to make yourself available without being overly involved in every fear. Example:

If your child is anxious about going to a birthday party, you might say, “It’s okay to feel nervous about meeting new people. I’ll be here to check in if you need me, but I think you’ll have fun once you’re inside.” Offer reassurance without hovering, which helps them feel supported yet capable.

By using calming phrases, thoughtful conversation techniques, and balanced validation, you can transform the way you communicate with your child during times of anxiety. These tools will not only ease their immediate worries but also build their confidence and ability to handle challenges over time. With your steady, calm approach, your child can learn that anxiety doesn’t have to overwhelm them. It’s something they can face, manage, and eventually overcome.

Step 3 – Supporting Emotional Resilience

Helping children build emotional resilience is one of the most valuable steps you can take to support their well-being. Emotional resilience is the ability to manage big feelings, bounce back from struggles, and adapt to life's challenges. It's not about suppressing emotions but learning how to process and work through them effectively. This chapter provides simple, practical ways to nurture your child's ability to face their worries and grow stronger through challenges.

Naming and Normalizing Feelings

For many kids, anxiety feels overwhelming because they don't fully understand what they're experiencing. Teaching them to name and normalize their feelings is the first step in helping them feel more in control.

Why Naming Feelings Helps

When children can label an emotion, it becomes less scary. Instead of being swept away by "bad" feelings, they can pinpoint whether they're feeling nervous, sad, frustrated, or excited. This awareness gives them a starting point for working through their emotions.

How Parents Can Help

1. ***Model it in everyday situations***

   Use your own experiences to teach emotional vocabulary. For example, you might say, "I'm feeling a little stressed because I have a big meeting today, but I know I'll feel better after I've prepared." Hearing you name your feelings shows kids it's normal and okay to experience a range of emotions.

2. ***Use tools to explore feelings***

   Create a feelings chart with different emotions paired with facial expressions. Ask questions like, "Which one of these faces matches how you feel right now?" or "Where do you feel this in your body?"

3. ***Validate their emotions***

   Avoid dismissing or minimizing their concerns. Instead of saying, "There's nothing to be worried about," you can try, "It sounds like you're feeling worried right now. That's a hard feeling, but I'll help you through it." This reassures them that their feelings are accepted and understood.

4. *Normalize Through Repetition*

   Help your child understand that everyone experiences feelings like fear, anger, or sadness. Share relatable stories, such as characters from books or TV shows, who face and overcome challenges. When kids realize their emotions are shared and normal, it reduces the power those feelings hold.

Gentle Exposure and "Brave Moments"

Avoiding anxiety triggers might feel like protecting your child, but over time, avoidance can make their fears grow. Instead, encourage gentle exposure to help them build bravery in manageable steps.

What is Gentle Exposure?

Gentle exposure means gradually helping your child face fears in small, achievable ways, allowing them to experience success without feeling overwhelmed. This builds their confidence and reduces their overall anxiety over time.

How to Create "Brave Moments"

1. *Start small*

   Break challenges into bite-sized steps. For example, if your child fears dogs, start by looking at pictures of dogs, then move to watching one from a distance, and eventually meeting a calm, friendly dog.

2. ***Celebrate effort, not outcome***

   Focus on the attempt, not the result. Whether or not your child achieves the goal doesn't matter as much as trying. For example, praise them by saying, "You were so brave to try talking to the cashier!"

3. ***Use a bravery jar***

   For each "brave moment," add a token, bead, or sticker to a jar. This visual reminder shows them the progress they're making and keeps them motivated to try again.

Provide support, but don't force exposure beyond what your child can handle. Their willingness to take brave steps comes more easily when they feel safe and supported by you.

Calming Tools: Breathing, Movement, and Sensory Play

Teaching your child calming tools helps them regulate their emotions in real-time. This gives them practical ways to manage anxiety when it pops up.

Breathing Techniques

Simple breathing exercises can quickly calm the nervous system. Here are a few easy methods to try with your child:

1. ***Balloon Breaths***: Ask your child to imagine their belly is a balloon. They "blow it up" with a big inhale and "deflate it" with a slow exhale. Repeat this 3–5 times.
2. ***Flower and Candle Breathing***: Pretend to smell a flower with a deep inhale, then blow out a candle with a long, gentle exhale. This exercise is fun and easy to follow.
3. ***Counting to Slow Down***: Encourage your child to breathe in slowly for a count of four and then exhale for a count of six. Counting makes them focus, which distracts from their worries.

Movement for Emotional Release

Physical activity can help kids release pent-up anxiety. Even a few minutes of movement engages their body and mind, providing an outlet for stress.

- ***Dance Party***: Put on music and dance freely. It's fun and spontaneous!
- ***Yoga for Kids***: Simple poses like child's pose or downward dog help stretch and relax muscles.
- ***Jump or Shake***: Encourage jumping, stomping, or shaking their hands like a wiggle worm to shake off tension.

Sensory Play to Soothe

Engaging the senses can ground anxious thoughts and refocus your child's attention.

- ***Touch***: Play with kinetic sand, stress balls, or soft blankets.
- ***Sight***: Watch a calming glitter jar or enjoy an outdoor view like the sky.
- ***Sound***: Listen to nature sounds, quiet music, or a favorite audiobook.
- ***Smell***: Use soothing scents like lavender during bedtime routines.

Build a Calm Toolkit

Create a "calm kit" with items your child can use when they feel tense. Include things like a favorite stuffed animal, a coloring book, fidget toys, or a bottle of bubbles for mindful breathing. Knowing this kit is always available provides reassurance.

Supporting your child's emotional resilience takes patience, but the payoff is invaluable. When you help them name and accept their feelings, take brave little steps, and use tools to calm themselves, you're equipping them with skills they'll carry for life. These practices not only help manage anxiety but also strengthen your bond, showing your child that they can count on you as their biggest cheerleader along the way.

Step 4 – Managing Screen Time and Stimulation

Screens are a double-edged sword for families. While they offer learning opportunities and entertainment, they can also lead to overstimulation, heightened anxiety, and disrupted balance in daily life. This chapter lays out how to recognize the effects of overstimulation, set boundaries that reduce conflict, and find screen-free activities that promote calm and connection.

How Overstimulation Fuels Anxiety

Screens provide endless access to games, videos, and social content, but too much stimulation can overwhelm a child's developing brain. Each notification, video, and interactive game hits the brain with a dopamine rush, keeping kids hooked while also draining their mental and emotional reserves.

Signs of Overstimulation

Your child might be struggling with overstimulation if you notice:

- Mood swings: Irritability or frequent meltdowns after screen time.
- Trouble transitioning: Resistance to stop using screens or move on to other tasks.
- Sleep issues: Difficulty falling or staying asleep due to excessive screen exposure, particularly before bedtime.
- Physical symptoms: Headaches or eye strain from extended digital use.
- Hyperfocus or withdrawal: Your child may become zoned out or overly attached to devices.

Why This Fuels Anxiety

Over time, overstimulation taxes the nervous system, making it harder for your child to unwind and self-regulate. The fast-paced, flashy content doesn't just affect their attention span; it also keeps their cortisol and adrenaline levels elevated. When this becomes the norm, children may begin to feel more anxious, irritable, and unable to cope with everyday stressors.

Recognizing the impact of overstimulation is the first step toward helping your child feel more balanced.

Sample Tech Boundaries Without Drama

Setting screen-time limits is crucial, but the process doesn't have to lead to constant battles. The key is creating boundaries that feel fair and consistent, minimizing those endless negotiations that drain everyone's energy.

Tips for Setting Tech Boundaries

1. **Define "screen-free zones"**

   Identify areas in your home where devices aren't allowed, such as the dinner table, bedrooms, or during family activities. These zones promote healthier interactions and reduce overstimulation before bedtime.

2. **Use timers instead of arguments**

   Set a physical timer or rely on tech settings to automatically turn off devices after the allotted time. This takes the emotional weight off you and reinforces that limits are non-negotiable.

   Example: "You can watch 30 minutes of YouTube after homework, and when the timer goes off, it's time to switch to a screen-free activity."

3. **Set "power-down" hours**

   Establish a daily cutoff time for screens, especially in the evening. For example, screens off an hour before bedtime ensures your child winds down naturally and prepares their brain for sleep.

4. **Collaborate on rules**

   Engage your child in creating family screen-time rules so they feel invested in the process. Ask questions like,

"How do you think we can balance fun and other activities?" This invites cooperation and understanding.

5. **Stay consistent**

   Stick to the boundaries you set, even if resistance arises. Your calm and steady response ("I know stopping now is tough, but this is the rule we agreed on") reinforces that these limits are for everyone's well-being.

What If They Push Back?

Validate their emotions while holding your ground. For instance, "I see that you're upset about turning it off. I know it's hard, but you've been on for a while, and it's time for a break." Calm, empathetic communication defuses power struggles over time.

Alternatives That Regulate

Screen-free time doesn't mean just removing devices; it's about replacing that time with activities that nourish your child's body and mind. Offering restorative alternatives is key to fostering balance.

Ideas for Screen-Free Activities That Encourage Calm

1. ***Creative Play***: Encourage unstructured play that sparks imagination while keeping overstimulation at bay. This

could include building with LEGO, painting, crafting, or pretend play.

2. ***Outdoor Adventures***: Nature has a calming effect on kids (and adults). Regular outdoor time can help reset their nervous system. Go for a walk, plant flowers in the garden, or play an easy game like tag or hide-and-seek.
3. ***Physical Movement***: Incorporate activities like biking, dancing, or kids' yoga to release built-up energy. Physical outlets also boost mood and promote better sleep.
4. ***Sensory-Based Relaxation***: Provide options like kinetic sand, water play, or a sensory bin filled with items to explore. These activities engage their senses, helping them feel grounded.
5. ***Family Bonding***: Strengthen your connection as a family with activities like board games, storytelling, or cooking together. Even low-key activities like puzzles can be great for stress relief.

Create a Balanced Daily Rhythm

Having a predictable routine that blends screen time with enriching screen-free breaks supports your child's anxiety management. For example:

- Morning routine includes offline "wake-up" activities like breakfast and stretching.

- Limited screen time during downtime (e.g., after school for 30 minutes).
- Evening family time where everyone disconnects from devices together.

Be Flexible with Transitions

Transitioning away from screens is easier when you prepare your child in advance. Use reminders like, “You have 10 minutes left on the iPad, and then we’re switching to reading time.” Positive reinforcement helps, too! Praise them when they follow the boundaries, e.g., “You stopped right when the timer buzzed. Awesome job listening!”

While managing screen time and addressing overstimulation may feel like a big hurdle, introducing clear boundaries and structured alternatives provides a smoother path. Your child will learn to self-regulate, engage in fulfilling activities, and build healthier habits. With time and consistency, this step helps reduce anxiety and create a calmer rhythm for your family.

Step 5 – Creating a Family Calm Culture

A peaceful family culture forms the foundation for managing your child's anxiety and screen time. By fostering calm within the home, you provide a steady anchor for your child in an often chaotic world. This chapter explores how parents can lead by example, rework patterns of conflict, and make small yet impactful shifts to nurture a tranquil environment where everyone can thrive.

Modeling Self-Regulation as a Parent

Children learn a great deal from how their parents handle stress. If you can manage your emotions effectively, you show your child that self-regulation is possible, even during difficult moments.

Why Modeling Matters

Kids are natural observers. They see how you react when the unexpected happens, like running late or dealing with a frustrating situation. By staying calm, you're teaching them that emotions, even strong ones, don't have to dominate our actions.

Practical Ways to Model Calm

1. ***Narrate your self-regulation process***

   When you feel stressed, verbalize how you're managing it. For example, "I'm feeling really upset right now, so I'm going to take a few deep breaths to help myself feel better." This kind of modeling teaches your child what to do when they face big emotions.

2. ***Use calming tools yourself***

   Whether it's practicing mindfulness, going for a quick walk, or writing in a journal, showing that you actively engage with calming activities reinforces their importance.

3. ***Own your mistakes***

   If you lose your temper, acknowledge it. Say something like, "I'm sorry for yelling earlier. I felt overwhelmed, but I should have handled that better. Next time, I'll try to pause before reacting." This demonstrates accountability and shows that mistakes are part of learning.

You can't pour from an empty cup. Prioritize your mental and physical health by carving out time for activities that recharge you, whether it's exercising, calling a friend, or simply getting a good night's sleep. When you take care of yourself, you reinforce the message that emotional health is important for everyone in the family.

Reworking Conflict Cycles

Families naturally experience disagreements, but unresolved or frequent conflict can create tension that heightens anxiety for everyone, particularly children. Learning how to approach conflicts calmly and constructively can transform the energy of your home.

The Four Steps to Mending Conflict Cycles

1. **Pause before reacting**

   When emotions run high, it's easy to say or do something you regret. Instead, take a moment to pause, take a few breaths, and consider your response. This will create space to respond thoughtfully rather than react impulsively.

   Example: If your child yells during a heated argument, resist the urge to yell back. Instead, calmly say, "I hear that you're upset. Can we talk about this when we're both feeling calmer?"

2. **Use "I" statements**

   When discussing an issue, frame your feelings as your own instead of placing blame. For example, "I feel frustrated when bedtime is ignored because it throws off the evening" is more productive than, "You never listen at bedtime."

3. **Repair after rupture**

   Conflict is inevitable, but repairing the damage afterward is essential. Apologize and acknowledge each person's feelings after an argument. This helps rebuild trust and shows your child it's okay to make amends.

4. **Create problem-solving habits**

   Instead of focusing only on the disagreement, involve your child in finding solutions. Ask, "What do you think we can do differently next time?" Collaborative problem-solving strengthens mutual respect and builds resilience for future challenges.

Avoid Common Conflict Triggers

While no family is conflict-free, you can minimize unnecessary friction by addressing recurring stress points. For example:

- ***Overbooked schedules***: Limit commitments to avoid overtired and stressed-out family members.

- ***Unclear rules***: Clearly define expectations for chores, screen time, and shared spaces to reduce confusion and arguments.

Simple Shifts for a Peaceful Home Tone

Transforming your home doesn't require drastic changes. Small, deliberate shifts in how you engage with your family can foster a more relaxing atmosphere that benefits everyone.

Bring Mindfulness Into the Home

1. ***Daily reset rituals***: Implement simple moments of calm into the daily rhythm, like five minutes of deep breathing before dinner or a quiet morning stretch together.
2. ***Practice gratitude***: Keep a family gratitude jar where everyone can write down one positive thing about their day. Read these together weekly to focus on shared joys.

Prioritize Positive Interactions

Aim for a 5-to-1 ratio of positive interactions to corrections or criticisms. This means focusing on efforts like, "You worked really hard on that homework!" instead of constantly pointing out mistakes. Acknowledging the good creates a lighter, more encouraging tone in your home.

Declutter Stress from Your Environment

A soothing space can go a long way in easing tension. Here's how:

- Minimize visual clutter: Tidy up common areas to reduce overstimulation.
- Use calming decor: Add soft lighting, cozy blankets, or peaceful elements like houseplants or family photos to encourage relaxation.
- Quiet zones: Set up quiet areas where your child can go to decompress.

Protect Family Connection Time

Even 10–15 minutes of undivided attention per child daily can strengthen bonds and create a atmosphere of security. Use this time to:

- Read a favorite book together.
- Play a short board game or do a puzzle.
- Simply talk and listen about their day.

Encourage Laughter and Play

A lighthearted approach goes a long way in promoting calm. Turn small moments into opportunities for joy, whether it's cracking a joke or doing a silly dance. Play helps everyone in the family reset and find ease in each other's company.

Creating a calm family culture doesn't mean you'll never have tough days, but it does ensure your home becomes a buffer against outside stressors. When you model self-regulation, approach conflict with care, and make small shifts to foster connection, you provide your child with both the tools and the example they need to face life's challenges with resilience and security.

When to Seek Extra Support

Supporting your child through anxiety and managing screen time at home is a powerful way to promote their well-being, but there may be times when outside help is necessary. This chapter helps you recognize when it's time to seek additional support, how to work collaboratively with professionals like schools and therapists, and how to approach advocacy with confidence and without shame.

What's Normal vs. When to Get Help

Anxiety is a normal and natural emotion, but the line between typical worry and an issue needing intervention can sometimes feel blurry. Understanding what's age-appropriate and when to take action is crucial in ensuring your child gets the support they need.

Normal Anxiety by Age

Children often experience fears and worries that align with their developmental stages. For example:

- ***Preschoolers***: Fear of monsters, darkness, or being apart from parents.

- ***School-age kids***: Worry about school performance, making friends, or family members' safety.
- ***Teenagers***: Anxiety around self-image, social dynamics, or the future.

These worries typically resolve with reassurance, time, and support.

Signs It's Time to Seek Help

Consider reaching out for professional support if:

1. ***The anxiety interferes with daily life***: Your child avoids activities they previously enjoyed, refuses to go to school, or has difficulty completing regular tasks.
2. ***Physical symptoms persist***: Chronic headaches, stomachaches, or other stress-related symptoms are common red flags.
3. ***Sleep patterns are disrupted***: Trouble falling or staying asleep, or constant exhaustion due to worry.
4. ***Intense emotional reactions***: Frequent meltdowns, anger outbursts, or shutting down completely in response to challenges.
5. ***Avoidance becomes a pattern***: Your child consistently avoids situations or people out of fear.

If you've tried the strategies in this guide and your child still struggles, seeking professional assistance can provide them (and you) with additional tools to move forward.

Working with Schools and Therapists

Schools and mental health professionals can play key roles in helping your child manage anxiety. Collaboration ensures your child gets comprehensive support across different parts of their life.

How to Approach Schools for Support

1. ***Start with the teacher***: If school difficulties fuel your child's anxiety, reach out to their teacher first. Share your observations and ask if they've noticed similar behaviors in the classroom. Teachers can often adjust environments or approaches to better meet your child's needs.
2. ***Request a meeting***: If challenges persist, ask for a meeting with the school counselor, special education coordinator, or administrative team.

   Discuss potential accommodations like:

   - Extra time for tests or assignments.
   - A quiet place for breaks when feeling overwhelmed.
   - Reduced workload during high-stress periods.

3. ***Key documentation***: If your child has a diagnosed anxiety disorder or related challenge, inquire about creating a 504 Plan or Individualized Education

Program (IEP) that outlines specific supports they'll receive at school.

Finding and Working with a Therapist

1. ***Choosing a therapist***: Look for professionals specializing in childhood anxiety. Therapies like cognitive-behavioral therapy (CBT) are evidence-based and highly effective in helping kids develop tools to manage their worries.
2. ***Prepare your child***: Frame therapy as a positive resource, using age-appropriate language. For example, you could say, "We're going to meet someone who's really good at helping kids learn new ways to feel calm and confident."
3. ***Stay involved***: Attend parent-focused sessions when possible, and maintain open communication with the therapist. This ensures the strategies used in therapy align with your family's home approach.
4. ***Be patient***: Change takes time. Progress may be gradual, with some ups and downs along the way. Celebrate small wins and trust that professional guidance is helping your child strengthen their coping skills.

How to Advocate Without Shame

Seeking extra support can be challenging, particularly when feelings of guilt or worry about judgment arise. Moving past these barriers is essential to getting the help your child needs.

1. **Recognize That Asking for Help is Strength**

   It can be easy to feel that asking for help means you're failing as a parent. The truth is, taking this step is one of the most proactive and loving things you can do. You're demonstrating to your child that it's okay to ask for assistance and that they're never alone in their struggles.

2. **Build a Team Around Your Child**

   You don't have to do this alone. Support from teachers, therapists, family members, and even friends creates a network that uplifts you and your child during hard times.

3. **Talk Openly About Your Concerns**

   When discussing your child with others, such as teachers or therapists, be frank about what you're seeing. Instead of worrying about judgement, approach the situation with the mindset that you're all there to work toward a common goal.

4. **Replace Shame with a Growth Mindset**

   View these challenges as opportunities to learn and grow together. Progress isn't about perfection but persistence. By seeing help as a tool rather than a weakness, you set a powerful example for your child.

Parenting is a journey, and there are times when seeking professional or external support is the right decision. Recognizing when your child's anxiety is beyond what they can handle alone, working collaboratively with schools and therapists, and advocating without shame provides them with the foundation they need to overcome obstacles. It also reinforces the message that they are surrounded by people who care about and believe in their ability to thrive.

Your 30-Day Family Calm Plan

When life feels chaotic and anxiety takes hold, it's easy to feel overwhelmed. But meaningful change doesn't happen in a single day; it's the result of consistent, little steps over time. This 30-day plan is designed to help your family transition into a calmer, more connected rhythm. Each week builds on the last, offering practical, manageable goals that you can tailor to your family's needs.

Remember, progress—not perfection—is the goal. Some days won't go as planned, and that's okay. What matters most is showing up and continuing to nurture a steady, calming environment.

Weekly Mini Goals

Week 1: Establish Anchoring Routines

Routine anchors, such as consistent morning and bedtime habits, provide a sense of stability and trust. For children, predictable routines are like lighthouses in their day, signaling safety and structure amidst life's uncertainties. This week's focus is on creating these anchors to foster a secure and predictable rhythm for your child.

Morning Routine

Mornings set the tone for the entire day. A predictable flow keeps stress and chaos to a minimum while giving your child a strong start.

Key Steps for a Morning Routine:

1. ***Set a Consistent Wake-Up Time***: Choose a wake-up time that works for your family and stick to it daily, even on weekends. Consistency regulates your child's internal body clock, making mornings smoother and sleep patterns healthier.

   Example: If school starts at 8 AM, waking your child by 6:30 or 7 AM allows enough time for a calm, unhurried morning.

2. ***Create a Simple Flow***: Develop a manageable step-by-step routine that's easy for kids to follow. Each step acts as a cue for what's next, leaving no room for guesswork.

   A flow could look like this:

   - Wake up.
   - Use the bathroom and brush teeth.

- Get dressed (clothes can be chosen the night before).
- Sit down for breakfast.

Spend a moment together reviewing the day. Ask questions like, ***"What are you excited about today?"*** or ***"What's one thing you want to focus on?"*** This promotes mindfulness and prepares them emotionally.

3. ***Reduce Morning Stress by Prepping the Night Before***: Avoid rushed mornings by handling essential tasks ahead of time:
    - Lay out clothes for the next day.
    - Pack lunches and snacks.
    - Ensure school bags are ready by the door with any required homework, projects, or supplies.

Additional Tips for Morning Success:

- Add a moment of connection, like a morning hug or a quick chat, to start the day on a positive note. Connection helps reduce anxiety and builds emotional safety.
- Avoid overwhelming your child with too many morning responsibilities. Keep it simple and direct. Don't overload them with chores or non-urgent decisions like choosing breakfast options on the fly.

Bedtime Routine

Bedtimes are crucial for emotional decompression and physical health. A calming routine helps kids transition from the energy of the day to restful sleep, allowing their bodies and brains to recharge.

Key Steps for a Bedtime Routine:

1. ***Decide on a Fixed Bedtime***

   Determine what time your child needs to fall asleep to get 8–10 hours of rest, depending on their age. Work backward to set when the bedtime routine should start.

   Example: If they need to wake up at 7 AM, aim for lights out by 8–9 PM at the latest. Start winding down 30–60 minutes before this.

2. ***Calming Activities Before Bed***

   Introduce a few quiet, soothing activities to signal it's time to relax. Options include:

   - Reading a favorite book together.
   - Listening to soft music or nature sounds.
   - Sharing three things each family member feels thankful for that day. This gratitude practice helps end the day on a positive note.

3. ***Dim the Lights***: Lower lighting in the hour before bed to help encourage natural melatonin production,

signaling the body it's time to sleep. Nightlights for younger kids can add comfort.

4. ***Limit Screen Use***: No screens in the hour leading up to bedtime. The blue light disrupts sleep by interfering with the body's internal signals for winding down. Instead, encourage alternative activities, like drawing, puzzles, or storytelling.

Additional Tips for Bedtime Success:

- Incorporate tactile comfort like soft blankets, cuddly toys, or a gentle back rub.
- If your child expresses worries or stress during this time, encourage them to voice their feelings, but avoid lengthy problem-solving. Offer reassurance like, "I'm here, and we'll figure it out together tomorrow."

Morning and bedtime anchors provide your child with predictable moments of connection and care. These structured patterns reduce the mental energy required to process what's happening next, allowing your child to focus on what truly matters throughout the day.

Week 2: Introduce Screen Time Boundaries

Screens are often a double-edged sword. They can entertain and educate but also overstimulate and create family tension over usage limits. This week's goal is to set clear, balanced boundaries that support your child's well-being without escalating frustration or power struggles.

Define Screen-Free Zones

Designating areas of your home as screen-free creates natural boundaries around when and where technology is used. These spaces can promote connection, relaxation, or focus.

1. ***Example of Screen-Free Zones***:
    - The dining table, to encourage meaningful conversations during meals.
    - Bedrooms, to improve sleep hygiene and create a calming, screen-free retreat.
    - Family living spaces during specific times, such as game or story nights.

2. ***How to Implement***:
    - Make it a family decision. Clearly explain the "why" of screen-free zones, such as promoting better sleep or bonding time.
    - Use physical reminders if needed, like a small sign or a designated box for devices.

Set Screen Time Windows

Rather than restricting screens all day, designate specific times when devices can be used. This promotes moderation and balance without screens becoming the "default" activity.

1. ***Examples of Screen Time Windows***:
    - After homework is completed on weekdays.
    - Two-hour blocks on weekends for gaming or watching shows.
    - No screens an hour before or after meals.
2. ***Practical Tools to Enforce Limits***:
    - Use a timer or device settings to alert kids when their time is running out.
    - Encourage them to plan what they want to watch or play ahead of time to ensure they use their time wisely.

Model Healthy Boundaries

Kids learn from what they see. If you're constantly scrolling through social media or answering work emails during family time, they notice. Use this week to model the behavior you want to see in your children by being mindful of your own screen use.

<u>Practical Strategies:</u>

- Keep your phone out of sight during meals or family conversations.
- Share a family "unplug" plan, such as putting devices in a shared charging station after 7 PM.
- Talk about why these changes matter. For example, "I'm putting my phone away because I want to give you my full attention."

Focus on Screen-Free Alternatives

Introducing fun, engaging activities makes screen time reduction easier. Kids are more likely to stay off devices if they have exciting options.

Examples of Screen-Free Alternatives:

- Arts and crafts projects like painting or DIY slime-making.
- Physical activities like riding bikes, jumping rope, or playing catch.
- Family activities like board games, trivia, or cooking a meal together.

Setting boundaries around screen time teaches kids self-regulation and healthy habits. Balanced screen use encourages them to explore other forms of entertainment, connection, and relaxation while limiting the anxiety that overstimulation can cause.

Week 3: Practice Calming Communication

How you speak to your child can directly affect their emotional regulation. Words can either escalate a stressful moment or help defuse it, so this week's focus is on shifting how you listen and respond. Calming communication isn't about perfection or avoiding difficult topics; it's about creating a space where your child feels heard, supported, and emotionally safe.

Daily Check-Ins

Check-ins are a simple yet powerful way to connect with your child and show them that their feelings matter. When kids feel seen and understood, their stress levels often drop, and their ability to open up grows.

1. ***Set Aside 5–10 Minutes Daily***: Choose a consistent time, such as after school or before bedtime, to check in. Create a quiet environment free from distractions so your child knows they have your full attention.
2. ***Ask Open-Ended Questions***: Help your child reflect and express themselves without the pressure of a yes/no response.
    - Instead of "Did you have a good day?" try, "What was the best part of your day?"
    - Rather than "Do you feel okay?" ask, "What's something that made you feel happy or frustrated today?"
3. ***Show Empathy in Your Reactions***: Stay curious rather than dismissive, even if your child's feelings seem small to you. For example:
    - Child: "I felt left out at recess today."
    - Parent (calming response): "That sounds tough. Feeling left out can really hurt. Do you want to talk about it more?"

These moments of undivided attention strengthen your bond and teach your child that their emotions are valid and manageable.

Use Calming Phrases

Sometimes, the words we use unintentionally add to a child's anxiety. Phrases like "You're overreacting" may feel practical but can come across as dismissive. This week, focus on calming responses that validate your child's experience while helping them find solutions.

Examples of Calming Phrase Swaps:

- Instead of "You're overreacting," try, "I can see this is really hard for you. I'm here to help."
- Replace "Stop worrying" with, "It's okay to feel nervous. What's one step we can take together?"
- Swap "There's nothing to be upset about" for, "It's okay to feel this way. Do you want to talk about it?"

These small changes create a sense of emotional safety, helping your child feel understood rather than judged.

Model Emotional Regulation

Kids learn how to handle stress by observing the adults around them. If you respond to frustration with yelling or avoidance, they're likely to mimic that behavior. This week, practice modeling calm responses in challenging moments.

Tips for Modeling Emotional Regulation:

1. ***Name Your Own Feelings Out Loud***: Example: "I'm feeling really frustrated right now because we're running late. I'm going to take a deep breath to calm down."
2. ***Describe What You're Doing to Cope***: When you show your child how to manage emotions constructively, it gives them tools they can use themselves.

   Example: "I'm feeling a little stressed, so I'm going to step outside for some fresh air and come back ready to talk."

3. ***Repair After Tough Moments***: If you lose your temper, apologize and explain what you'll do differently.

   Example: "I'm sorry I yelled earlier. I was feeling overwhelmed. Next time, I'll try to pause before reacting."

By being open and honest about your emotions, you teach your child that feelings, even big ones, are okay and manageable.

Week 4: Strengthen Connection Through Family Bonding

The final week focuses on creating moments that bring your family closer together. These bonding activities don't have to be big or elaborate; they're about making time to connect through shared fun, laughter, and reflection. Reinforce the progress you've made with simple rituals that help everyone feel supported and loved.

Family Activity Day

Making time to do something fun as a family helps create positive memories and reduces stress for everyone. Shared activities promote teamwork, build trust, and remind kids that they're part of a supportive team.

How to Plan a Family Activity Day:

1. ***Pick One Day Each Week***: Choose a time when everyone can be present. Sundays or Saturday afternoons often work well.
2. ***Rotate Activity Choices***: Give each family member a turn to choose the activity. This ensures everyone feels included and heard.

   Examples of Activities:

   - A nature hike or trip to a nearby park.
   - Baking cookies or trying a new recipe together.
   - Family board game or card night.

- An arts and crafts project like painting or making holiday decorations.

3. ***Keep It Simple and Fun***: The focus is on connection, not perfection.

Tips for busy families: If you're short on time, even a 30-minute activity like a backyard picnic can create meaningful moments.

Start a Daily Gratitude Practice

Gratitude helps shift focus from what's gone wrong to what's going right. When practiced regularly, it can reframe the way your family views challenges and encourages positivity.

How to Introduce Gratitude:

1. ***Choose the Right Time***: During dinner or as part of the bedtime routine works well.
2. ***Model First***: Share your own gratitude to inspire your child.

   Example: "Today, I'm grateful for the sunny weather and the time we got to spend outside together."

3. ***Ask Specific Questions***: Broad prompts like **"What are you thankful for?"** can feel overwhelming. Try, **"What's one thing today that made you smile?"** or **"What's something kind someone did?"**

4. ***Make It Fun***: Younger kids might enjoy drawing their gratitude on paper or placing "thankful notes" into a jar.

Over time, this practice can help your family see and celebrate the bright spots in their days, even during difficult times.

Celebrate Successes

End the month by reflecting on all the progress you've made together. Celebrating small wins reinforces positive habits and gives everyone a sense of accomplishment.

Ideas for Celebrating Successes:

- Look back on the routines or boundaries you've implemented. Share stories about what's working well.
- Plan a small family reward, like a movie night with homemade popcorn, a favorite takeout meal, or an outing to a local park or ice cream shop.
- Offer verbal encouragement. Say things like, "I've noticed how much calmer our mornings are now," or "I'm so proud of how we've worked together as a family."

Celebrations reinforce that your efforts are paying off and motivate everyone to keep building on this new foundation.

Practical Tracker Templates

Using a tracker can help your family stay consistent and celebrate progress. Below are two example templates you can adapt to fit your needs.

Screen Time Tracker

Table 1: Screen Time Tracker (Sample)

Day	**Screen-Free Meals**	**Total Screen Time Hours**	**Did We Stick to Boundaries (Yes/No)**
Monday	Breakfast, Dinner	1.5	Yes
Tuesday	Breakfast	2	Yes
Wednesday	Dinner	2.5	No
Thursday	Dinner	1	Yes
Friday	Breakfast, Dinner	2	Yes

Table 2: Morning and Bedtime Routine Tracker for Kids (Sample)

Day	**Morning Steps Completed**	**Bedtime Steps Completed**	**Rate the Day (Smiley Face)**
Monday	3/3	3/3	😊
Tuesday	2/3	3/3	😊
Wednesday	3/3	2/3	😊

Thursday	3/3	3/3	😀
Friday	3/3	3/3	😀

Calming Communication Reflection (Parent Tracker)

Table 3: Parent Tracker (Sample)

Day	Emotionally Supportive Phrases Used	Did I Model Calm? (Yes/No)	What I Did Well
Monday	4	Yes	Used validating language
Tuesday	2	No	Paused before responding
Wednesday	3	Yes	Practiced empathic listening

These visual reminders motivate consistency and empower your child to take ownership of their habits.

How to Reset After a Hard Day

No family is perfect, and some days won't go as planned. Here's how to reset and gear up for a fresh start.

1. ***Pause and Regroup***: If the day felt chaotic, take time to pause. Acknowledge that it was tough, and remind yourself (and your kids) that tomorrow is a new opportunity.

2. ***Choose One Small Win***: Pick a single, achievable goal for the next day. For example, if bedtime fell apart, focus on sticking to the bedtime routine tomorrow rather than trying to overhaul everything at once.
3. ***Lean Into Connection***: After a stressful day, prioritize something that nurtures closeness. Share hugs, a favorite snack, or watch something lighthearted as a family. This reinforces that love and support are constant, even when things go wrong.
4. ***Practice Self-Compassion***: Parenting is hard work. Be gentle with yourself and model how to handle mistakes gracefully. Saying, "I had a hard day too, but I know we'll do better tomorrow," shows your child the importance of resilience and self-kindness.

The 30-day plan isn't about being perfect but about building routines, boundaries, and habits that lead to calm and connection over time. Celebrate the little wins, forgive the setbacks, and remember that creating a calmer family rhythm is a work in progress. You're doing an amazing job!

Conclusion

Parenting in today's fast-paced and often overstimulating world is anything but simple. Between managing your child's anxiety, navigating screen time, and juggling daily responsibilities, it's easy to feel overwhelmed. Yet, as you've seen throughout this guide, small, intentional steps can create big shifts—not just for your child's well-being but for the entire family.

One of the most crucial takeaways is that anxiety and screen time management doesn't need to be all or nothing. You don't have to overhaul your entire routine overnight. Instead, focus on incremental changes and celebrate progress no matter how small. Whether it's creating consistent morning anchors, modeling calming behaviors, or implementing screen-free zones, every step you take helps build a better rhythm within your home.

By understanding what anxiety looks like in children, you've equipped yourself to recognize the signs, even the hidden ones. When your child clings, avoids, or lashes out, you can now see beyond the behavior and address the emotions beneath. This insight alone empowers you to offer meaningful support rather than quick fixes. Remember, your role isn't to erase your child's anxiety but to help them face challenges with confidence. Encouragement and calm guidance teach resilience far better than removing every obstacle.

Screens, often seen as a critical pain point, can actually open the door to growth when managed thoughtfully. Setting technology boundaries doesn't need to stir constant conflict; instead, it's an opportunity to foster healthier habits and prioritize connection. By introducing alternatives like family game nights, creative projects, or outdoor adventures, you're helping your child (and yourself) reconnect in ways that matter.

Creating a family calm culture, as outlined in Step 5, takes patience and consistency. It's about intentional actions that reduce stress and strengthen relationships. Modeling emotional regulation, reworking conflict cycles, and weaving gratitude into your routines set a remarkable example. You're showing your child that even in overwhelming moments, calm is achievable, and home is a safe space.

Keep in mind that challenges will arise. There will be setbacks, tantrums, busy schedules that derail your efforts, and days when nothing seems to go as planned. That's normal. What matters most is how you respond. Give yourself the same grace you offer your child. If routines fall apart one day, reset the next. Progress is all about showing up, again and again.

Remember, you're not alone in this. There are moments when external support, like therapists or teachers, can provide valuable insights and tools. Seeking help when needed doesn't just benefit your child; it reinforces the message that growth is a team effort. You are their biggest advocate, and that advocacy is a gift.

This 30-day family calm plan is your companion, not a rigid rulebook. Personalize it to fit your family's needs, and don't hesitate to adjust along the way. With patience and intentionality, you're not only managing anxiety and screen time; you're cultivating resilience, connection, and harmony. One small change at a time, you're reshaping your home into a supportive haven where everyone, including you, can thrive. Take a deep breath and trust the process. You've got this.

FAQs

How can I tell if my child's behavior is linked to anxiety or just typical childhood stress?

Anxiety often goes beyond everyday stress and can interfere with your child's ability to enjoy daily activities. Signs of anxiety may include persistent worries, physical symptoms like headaches or stomachaches, trouble sleeping, clinginess, or irritability.

Younger kids might avoid new experiences, while older ones may withdraw or show perfectionistic tendencies. Pay close attention to recurring patterns and hidden signs like hypervigilance or difficulty concentrating. If these issues persist or disrupt your child's daily life, it's time to explore additional support.

What's the best way to reduce screen time without a daily power struggle?

The key to successfully reducing screen time lies in creating clear, consistent boundaries that feel fair to both you and your child. Start by setting specific screen-free zones (like during meals or in bedrooms) and designated "tech-off" times, such as an hour before bed.

Use timers to signal when screen time will end, and offer engaging alternatives like puzzles, outdoor play, or family activities. Staying calm and modeling healthy screen habits yourself will reinforce the message without unnecessary drama.

Can too much screen time make my child's anxiety worse?

Yes, screens can contribute to anxiety in several ways. Overstimulation from games, videos, or constant notifications keeps your child's brain on high alert, mimicking stress responses. Bright screens, especially before bedtime, interfere with sleep, which is crucial for emotional regulation.

Additionally, exposure to overwhelming or stressful content (like social media or the news) can heighten worries. Managing screen time and balancing it with calming activities is essential for reducing overstimulation and supporting your child's mental health.

What are some good screen-free activities that reduce anxiety?

Replacing screen time with enriching, calming activities helps kids regulate their emotions and reconnect with their surroundings. Some effective options include sensory play (like slime or kinetic sand), physical activities (such as biking or yoga), creative outlets (like drawing or crafting), outdoor time, and family bonding activities, like board games or storytelling. These alternatives engage your child's senses and imagination, encouraging relaxation and connection in place of digital distractions.

How can I help my child manage feelings of worry without over-focusing on their anxiety?

Start by validating their feelings with calm, empathetic phrases like, "I see this feels hard for you, but I'm here to help." Then, shift the focus to practical steps they can take to feel braver. For example, encourage deep breathing or simple problem-solving discussions.

Avoid dwelling on the details of what's making them anxious; instead, highlight their efforts and successes, which builds confidence over time. Balance support with teaching resilience so they feel empowered to handle their worries.

How can I create a calmer home environment to help reduce my child's anxiety?

Small changes can make a big difference. Establish consistent daily routines, especially at morning and bedtime, to provide a sense of predictability. Minimize visual and auditory clutter in your home and consider soft lighting or calming background music.

Foster connection through shared meals, gratitude practices, and quality one-on-one time. Redefine conflict cycles by modeling calm behavior and resolving disagreements constructively. These shifts create a sense of security and reduce overall family stress.

When should I seek professional help for my child's anxiety?

If your child's anxiety consistently interferes with their daily life—such as avoiding school, losing interest in activities they once loved, or experiencing chronic physical symptoms like stomachaches or headaches—it may be time to seek additional support.

Therapists who specialize in childhood anxiety can teach your child practical coping tools, while school counselors can offer accommodations to ease daily stressors. Don't hesitate to reach out; seeking help shows strength and commitment to your child's well-being.

References and Helpful Links

Anxiety in children. (2025, June 2). Cleveland Clinic. https://my.clevelandclinic.org/health/diseases/anxiety-in-children

Website, N. (2024, April 15). Anxiety in children. nhs.uk. https://www.nhs.uk/mental-health/children-and-young-adults/advice-for-parents/anxiety-in-children/#:~:text=From%20the%20age%20of%20around,around%20age%202%20to%203.

Paulson, D., PhD. (2022, July 14). 9 tools for helping your child manage anxiety. Mayo Clinic Health System. https://www.mayoclinichealthsystem.org/hometown-health/speaking-of-health/9-tools-for-helping-your-child-manage-anxiety

Goldstein, C., PhD. (2025, June 20). What to do (and not do) when children are anxious. Child Mind Institute. https://childmind.org/article/what-to-do-and-not-do-when-children-are-anxious/

Help your child manage anxiety: tips for home & school. (n.d.). HealthyChildren.org. https://www.healthychildren.org/English/family-life/family-dynamics/Pages/help-your-child-manage-fears-and-anxieties.aspx

Kids and anxiety: What's normal, what's not | Aetna. (n.d.). Aetna. https://www.aetna.com/health-guide/kids-anxiety-whats-normal-seek-help.html

Pagels, C. (2024, December 11). Supporting Children with Anxiety: A Guide for Parents. Mindpath Health. https://www.mindpath.com/resource/supporting-children-with-anxiety-a-guide-for-parents/

www.ingramcontent.com/pod-product-compliance
Lightning Source LLC
LaVergne TN
LVHW022020200926
848481LV00007B/2460
9798349523984